AF388542

Günter Kampf, MD

# The Stigmatisation of the Unvaccinated During COVID-19

Unpacking the Reactions to a Lancet Letter

**Imprint**

Bibliographic information of the German National Library: The German National Library lists this publication in the German National Bibliography; detailed bibliographic data is available on the Internet at http://dnb.dnb.de.

The automated analysis of the work in order to obtain information, in particular about patterns, trends and correlations in accordance with §44b UrhG ("Text and Data Mining") is prohibited.



Source of the cover image: Marta Nogueira by Pexels.

Publisher: BoD · Books on Demand GmbH, In de Tarpen 42, 22848 Norderstedt, Germany

Printed by: Libri Plureos GmbH, Friedensallee 273, 22763 Hamburg, Germany

ISBN: 978-3-7583-5147-1

# Foreword

To stigmatize people for health reasons has a long and ugly history. The Bible mentions how lepers were shunned by society, teaching us instead to show compassion and care. More recently, homosexual men with HIV/AIDS were stigmatized in the United States and around the world. An important principle of public health is that we care for everyone in a compassionate manner, irrespective of their health status or behavior. While public health should encourage people to stop smoking, we do not stigmatize them as being bad people and we do not deny them health care if they develop lung cancer. While we encourage healthy eating and exercise, we do not shame obese people or fire them from their work.

Among public health professionals, there used to be consensus that it was both unethical and counterproductive to stigmatize people, and most of the public agreed. That is, until the Covid pandemic threw this consensus out the window. When someone caught a Covid infection, they were often blamed for not being careful enough, not wearing a mask, for not socially distancing, for breaking lockdown rules or for not being vaccinated. This led in turn to social media posts where those with a recent Covid infection desperately tried to ensure their friends and followers that yes, they had taken all the required Covid precautions but got sick anyway.

Disturbed by all the stigma around Covid, in 2021 I posted the following on Twitter: *'For thousands of years, disease pathogens have spread from person to person.*

*Never before have carriers been blamed for infecting the next sick person. That is a very dangerous ideology.'* It got 14 million views and 9,400 comments. The second sentence is obviously untrue, and people jumped on it to point out that they were not the first ones to blame the sick. A few colleagues were more astute. Michael Senger tweeted that *"In a strange twist, blue-check Twitter mobbed @MartinKulldorff's tweet yesterday with tons of horrifying examples of infected persons being blamed, shamed, and ostracized in history—using those examples, bizarrely, to justify their own blaming of those infected with COVID."* Francois Balloux commented that my tweet *was 'either a complete brain fart or one of the most sophisticated examples of Socratic discourse. Whatever the intent, it got many to reflect on the abuse the most marginalised people in society experience during times of moral crisis. As such, it did its job.'*

The stigmatizing of the sick eventually stopped. Not because of my tweet, but because almost everyone eventually got Covid, no matter what precautions they took. People don't like blaming themselves, and how can you blame others for getting sick if you have also been sick?

One type of stigmatization was especially severe during the pandemic, and it has not yet ended. That is the stigmatization of the unvaccinated. Like the lepers in biblical times, the unvaccinated were shunned from society, not allowed to go to college, visit restaurants, attend cultural events, and in many cases, fired from their work. Putting aside the cruel and ugly aspects of this, it was also unscientific. The Covid vaccine trials had not shown that the vaccine would reduce transmission, and with a vaccine it can go either way. If the vaccine reduces symptomatic disease, infected persons may be more likely to spread it to others if they are vaccinated, as they will be out and about meeting other people, while unvaccinated people with symptoms stay at home in bed. Moreover, people who had recovered from a Covid infection already had natural immunity that was superior to the vaccinated, and with millions of unvaccinated high-risk people around the world due to vaccine shortage, it was unethical to vaccinate them. The same is true for young adults who were at miniscule risk of dying from Covid. Rather than stigmatizing them for not taking the vaccine, they should have been applauded for allowing older high-risk people to get the vaccine instead of them.

There were some attempts to counter the stigmatization of the unvaccinated. In The Lancet, Professor Günter Kampf published an important and well written piece, arguing that *'stigmatizing the unvaccinated is not justified'* and that it was inappropriate to use the term *'pandemic of the unvaccinated'*. This piece that should have been indisputable to everyone, turned out to be controversial, receiving an enormous amount of attention.

In this book, Dr. Kampf outlines some of the many reactions. In the past, stigmatizations often came from politicians, the media and segments of the public, with scientists and public health officials patiently and valiantly trying to counter it, knowing how unethical and counterproductive it is for public health. With the Covid vaccines, it was the other way around. It was public health officials and academics who were in the driving seat, pushing a destructive narrative that politicians, the media and some members of the public picked up on. That is a shocking and disturbing aspect of this stigmatization of the unvaccinated, and it will not go down well when the history of the Covid pandemic is written.

The positive aspect is that many people did not go along with it. This book is a beautiful testament to that. It is wonderful to read the many thoughtful and humane responses that Dr. Kampf received to his Lancet publication. It fills one with warmth and hope for the future.

Martin Kulldorff

# Table of contents

# 1. Background

The year 2021 was marked by the COVID-19 pandemic, not only in Germany. Probably the most moralised issue during the pandemic was the vaccination status. The moralising phrase 'pandemic of the unvaccinated' was coined early in the pandemic and quickly caught on. The idea that the pandemic had become more or less exclusively the domain of the unvaccinated has been persistent [1]. It was a time when politicians repeatedly made public statements about the dangers of unvaccinated people. Here are some examples.

**Joe Biden, President, USA**

"Look, the only pandemic we have is among the unvaccinated."

(17 July 2021; AP News)

**Janosch Dahmen, Green Party, Germany** (translated)

"Restrictive measures can only be justified if a group of people poses a danger. Vaccinated people are no longer a danger, so restrictions can no longer be applied to them."

(26 July 2021; ntv)

**Markus Söder, CSU, Germany** (translated)

"Anyone who has been vaccinated is not a danger, which is why their fundamental constitutional rights must be restored."

(10 August 2021; BR, Bayerischer Rundfunk)

Jennifer Russell, Chief Medical Officer, Canada

"This is a pandemic of the unvaccinated."

(2 September 2021; Toronto Star)

Jens Spahn, CDU, Germany (translated)

"We are currently seeing a pandemic of the unvaccinated."

(8 September 2021; DW, Deutsche Welle)

The public perception was clear: only the unvaccinated population was part of the pandemic, and only the unvaccinated population was able to transmit SARS-CoV-2 to contact persons so that the driver of the pandemic was the unvaccinated population. Very clear. They were to blame for the continuation of the pandemic. It was therefore only fair to impose restrictions on their public life, such as the 2G contact restrictions in Germany [2]. But was it that simple?

There was growing evidence that the vaccinated population was also infected and capable to transmit SARS-CoV-2 to contacts. Initially, it may have been true that the vaccinated were less likely to be infected and therefore less likely to be a possible source of transmission. But the black-and-white picture painted by some politicians was certainly wrong. And in October 2022, the protocols of the Robert Koch Institute even stated that there was no evidence that vaccinations make any difference to excretions [3].

Knowing this already in the autumn of 2021 motivated me to write a short piece about what I felt was an unjustified stigmatisation of the unvaccinated. According to the Cambridge Dictionary stigmatisation is "an act of treating someone or something unfairly by publicly disapproving them". I considered the public language described above as such.

I noticed in 2021 that public and private verbal interactions were more violent towards the unvaccinated. This experience was the other motivation for me to try to encourage all people to keep the society together.

## 2. The Lancet Letter

On 20 November 2021, my correspondence entitled "COVID-19: stigmatising the unvaccinated is not justified" was published in The Lancet [4]. The aim was to show that partially and fully vaccinated people can also be COVID-19 cases and therefore a possible source of transmission, and to emphasise that this was not a "pandemic of the unvaccinated". The stigmatisation of the unvaccinated population seen in many countries was, in my view, unjustified and therefore wrong. In addition, I also tried to encourage senior officials and scientists to stop the inappropriate stigmatisation of the unvaccinated and to make extra efforts to bring society together. Read the full correspondence here [4]:

*"In the USA and Germany, high-level officials have used the term pandemic of the unvaccinated, suggesting that people who have been vaccinated are not relevant in the epidemiology of COVID-19. Officials' use of this phrase might have encouraged one scientist to claim that "the unvaccinated threaten the vaccinated for COVID-19". But this view is far too simple.*

*There is increasing evidence that vaccinated individuals continue to have a relevant role in transmission. In Massachusetts, USA, a total of 469 new COVID-19 cases were detected during various events in July, 2021, and 346 (74%) of these cases were in people who were fully or partly vaccinated, 274 (79%) of whom were symptomatic. Cycle threshold values were similarly low between people who were fully vaccinated (median 22·8) and people who were unvaccinated, not fully vaccinated, or whose vaccination status was unknown (median 21·5), indicating a high viral load even among people who were fully vaccinated. In the USA, a total of 10 262 COVID-19 cases were reported in vaccinated people by April 30, 2021, of whom 2725 (26·6%) were asymptomatic, 995 (9·7%) were hospitalised, and 160 (1·6%) died. In Germany, 55·4% of symptomatic COVID-19 cases in patients aged 60 years or older were in fully vaccinated individuals, and this proportion is increasing each week. In Münster, Germany, new cases of COVID-19 occurred in at least 85 (22%) of 380 people who were fully vaccinated or who had recovered from COVID-19 and who attended a nightclub. People who are vaccinated have a lower risk of severe disease but are still a relevant part of the pandemic. It is therefore wrong and dangerous to speak of a pandemic of the unvaccinated. Historically, both the USA and Germany have engendered negative experiences by stigmatising parts of the population for their skin colour or religion. I call on high-level officials and scientists to stop the inappropriate stigmatisation of unvaccinated people, who include our patients, colleagues, and other fellow citizens, and to put extra effort into bringing society together."*

Altmetric publishes an 'attention score' for scientific articles. This article attracted an unusually high level of public attention with a score of 23,742. According to this evaluation, which extends to 30 September 2024, this letter to the editor is in the top 5% of all articles in all journals.

In the overall picture of all publications and all Lancet publications, the letter to the editor was ranked 17th and 2nd, respectively.

Figure 1: Screenshot of the Altimetric summary of the Lancet Letter (all publications) [5].

In the overall picture of all current publications and all current Lancet publications, the letter ranked #3 and #1, respectively. This makes it obvious that there was a great deal of international interest in this Lancet letter.

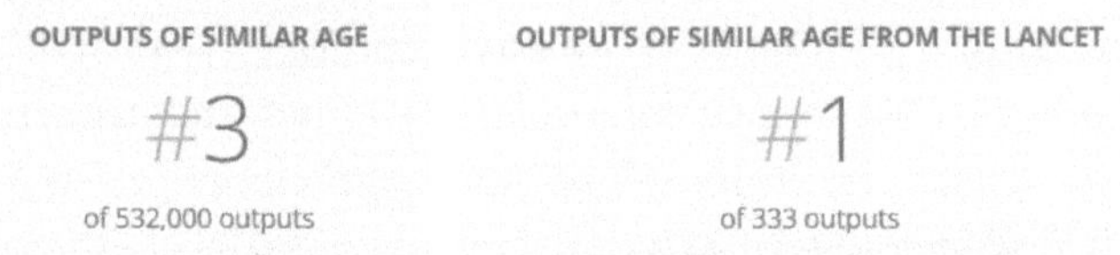


Figure 2: Screenshot of the Altimetric summary of the Lancet letter (current publications) [5].

Three years following the initial publication of my correspondence, I would like to disseminate the reactions I have received from the public. Within a two-month period, I received a total of 88 emails, a number unparalleled in my scientific career for any other publication. The diversity of these responses reflects a wide range of perspectives on the subject matter. It is my hope that publishing these responses will facilitate a critical evaluation of the pandemic measures, as well as the prevailing attitudes towards the unvaccinated population. Furthermore, I aim to address the behaviours of some academics in relation to the constitutionally protected academic freedom of science, and to highlight the statements made by key stakeholders that were often blunt and unjustified in 2021 regarding the unvaccinated.

## 3. Overview on reactions

I received a total of 88 responses, with the majority coming from laypeople (46.6%). The breakdown of other respondents is as follows: physicians (21.6%), university professors (9.1%), scientists (5.7%), nurses and students (3.4% each), and psychologists and lawyers (2.3% each). Additionally, I received responses from a pharmacist, a senator, a civil rights campaigner, a veterinary surgeon, an osteopath, and a PhD student, each contributing 1.1%. A representative from the University of Greifswald also sent me an email, this input will be covered separately in chapter 12.

Geographically, most responses were from Germany (40.9%), followed by the USA (9.1%), Canada and France (4.5% each), and Australia and the United Kingdom (3.4% each). Other countries represented included Ireland, Norway, Austria, and Italy (2.3% each), as well as Singapore, South Africa, Brazil, Spain, Bulgaria, Poland, and Belgium (1.1% each). The country of origin for 17.0% of the respondents remains unknown.

# 4. Reactions from citizens

This chapter contains 19 anonymized emails from citizens around the world to my letter to the editor in the Lancet. Their words shed light on the deep rifts in society and the importance of a nuanced, respectful approach to difficult issues.

### A citizen from Germany (translated)

"Even in my 'more' educated circle I see a blatant exclusion of people. I find it very surprising what rights some people give themselves."

### A citizen from Ireland

"I just wanted to say "thank you" for presenting the Science with integrity. It was good to read something that didn't vilify or scorn but just presented as it was."

### A citizen from Australia

"You are absolutely right. The vilification of the unvaccinated is divisive and absolute poison to any civilized society."

### A citizen from Germany (translated)

"I would like to thank you for this letter. It takes some courage to publish such a letter in these times. Over the past year and a half, I have been amazed by the phenomenon of how our society, in a kind of frenzy, without hesitation and without even realising it, is throwing overboard the values it once held. Since July (2021) at the latest, I also believe that politics has (finally) left the path of 'science' and rationality. I am very worried about where this will lead."

## A citizen

"I just wanted to thank you for writing your article published in the Lancet today. I appreciate you speaking out about this topic despite how risky it is to bring up. Courageous people like you are the kind of people that we need more of in the world."

## A citizen from Italy

"A choral thank you on my behalf and on behalf of the entire world population for your work and above all for your valuable article of 11/20/2021 on the Lancet."

## A citizen from Singapore

"Thank you for writing stigmatising the unvaccinated is not justified. Recently I met a lawyer who not just once but at least twice being very abusive. I lost that assignment and income. It's okay as I will not want to continue to work for such person."

## A citizen

"Thank you for your insightful article. I wonder is there an appetite for discussing the importance of a Green Pass/Covid Certificate in an article. It seems coverage of same is thin on the ground. I understand that Dr Fauci and others all seem to agree that all persons, regardless of their vaccination status, carry the same viral loads. Therefore, if the purpose of barring entry to various establishments is to stop the spread, then what do the said passes contribute to? I am truly interested and perhaps they have an important benefit and could this be discussed? I think we are all anxious to limit the effect of this contagious nasty virus and all hands should be on deck. As you point out, a combined effort, one that entails respect, kindness and empathy to one and all should be undertaken by each country."

## A citizen from South Africa

"I salute you! I have hope for humanity when I see people like you standing up for the truth. As MLK said: "In the end we will remember not the words of our enemies but the silence of our friends"."

## A citizen

"Thank you for speaking out. I agree 100%. For some reason, it is unpopular and even risky to do so. Shouldn't be that way. Thank you again for contributing to the discussion in a productive way."

## A citizen from Germany (translated)

"Thank you for your article in the Lancet 'COVID-19: stigmatising the unvaccinated is not justified'. You are helping to stop these metastases of discrimination and marginalisation in our society. I am writing this as a vaccinated person who considers the current development to be intolerable and highly dangerous for society and democracy. Even the data from the RKI (Robert Koch Institute; addition by the author) and the PEI (Paul Ehrlich Institute; addition by the author), which clearly show that the vaccination is neither sufficiently safe nor effective to the extent that it is being propagated, are almost completely ignored by politicians and the media. I wish you continued success and please continue to raise awareness!"

A citizen from Germany (translated)

"Unfortunately, opinions and voices like yours are not published in the public sphere because they say something other than what is probably intended to be disseminated. The 'scapegoat' for the 4th wave has been identified and that's how it should stay. It is not desirable for anyone to have to be treated in intensive care, regardless of the illness or health impairment. However, the 'unvaccinated' are certainly not to blame for the lack of beds in ICUs. There are probably other reasons for this, which should be of a financial nature."

A citizen from Germany (translated)

"I just wanted to say THANK YOU for your courageous statement in the Lancet. A differentiated recording of the current cases would be so urgently needed (1x vaccinated, 2x vaccinated, unvaccinated), but is omitted, as well as a breakdown into Covid as the main diagnosis and secondary diagnosis and much more. It is completely misleading to pillory the unvaccinated: Ethically anyway, but medically, because the vaccinated (especially through 2G) get a kind of free pass and this creates a huge blind spot (condoning acceptance??). I'll leave it at that (there would be infinitely more to say) and THANK YOU once again for your courage!!!"

## A citizen from Germany (translated)

"I would like to thank you very much for your courage and for your open letter published in The Lancet. The controversial discussion of this issue is unfortunately not something that can be taken for granted, so you speak to me and my family, and I am sure to many other people, from the heart. I would also like to thank you for taking a societal view. Alongside the discussion of the medical aspects, the human perspective is often forgotten and the fact that we all have to live together again at some point is somehow ignored. Statements like yours give us hope that humanity is not quite over after all."

## A citizen

"I read with appreciation your note to The Lancet and your call to stop the stigmatisation of unvaccinated people. This is a much-needed sentiment and I congratulate you for finding a high-profile chance to publicly express it. Best wishes for a saner world."

## A citizen

"I've just read all your articles in The Lancet and just wanted to say thank you for being a rational voice amongst a lot of irrational ones. I'm not a scientist but I can read research papers and since I studied psychology and statistics, I know how to interpret a lot of the results. What I've been reading has been very different to what the governments and media are saying. Your commentary and articles are very straightforward and easy to read and I will be sharing them with as many people as possible. Please keep up being the voice in this situation! It is so needed."

## A citizen from Canada

"I appreciate that you shared your views regarding stigmatizing unvaccinated people in The Lancet. I wish everyone would consider this perspective and look long and hard at how the current policies are shaping our world and our ability and right to make choices regarding our own bodies, our approach to health and that of our children. Thank you for your refreshing article amidst so much rhetoric. I understand there is misinformation being churned around on both "sides" of the equation. We can only hope and pray people start looking at how to unite and solve the world problems despite our differences."

## A citizen from Australia

"I recently read your paper regarding stigmatisation of the unvaccinated. An excellent illustration, in full support of what you have postulated, can be seen in the recent experience of South Australia where I live. Until the 25th November, 2021, South Australia had almost zero cases of SARS-II, having upheld strict border restrictions to other States, particularly those with high case numbers. On the 26th November 2021, however, it was decided to open borders to all States (including NSW and Victoria who at the time, were experiencing

1000 new daily cases - mostly delta). Most significantly, only 'vaccinated' people were allowed into South Australia from 26th November due to the supposed 'dangers' the unvaccinated posed to the rest of the community. Within days of borders opening, Covid case numbers escalated and continue to increase daily. We now have over 18,000 cases in South Australia. From Zero to 18,000 in just over a month, despite only 'vaccinated' people being allowed into the State. It appears to be the vaccinated who brought Covid into South Australia, not the unvaccinated. Is there actually any scientific proof that the unvaccinated are more 'contagious' or dangerous? Common sense tells me the opposite is true as Covid-positive unvaccinated people are likely to feel sick and stay home in bed, while the positive 'vaccinated' will either be asymptomatic or with only mild symptoms and therefore more likely to be out and about, spreading the disease in the community. Furthermore, many vaccinated are not bothering to wear their masks anymore "because they are vaccinated". In agreement with your research, the South Australian data shows that it is totally unjustified and terribly unfair to be stigmatising the unvaccinated, as is being done around the world. As the SA experience indicates, it appears to be the vaccinated who pose the greater danger of spread of this disease, not the unvaccinated. And whether vaccinated or not, the most logical deterrent to the spread of this virus is mask-wearing, given that both can catch and spread the virus. Whether you are vaccinated or not, should be declared irrelevant - as has been perfectly demonstrated in South Australia's example. Thank you for your work and publications. I look forward to reading more in future."

## A citizen from the UK

"I read your article in the Lancet and completely agree with it. Here in the UK, high level officials are saying the unvaccinated are burdening the healthcare system. I have never heard the same terminology being used for people who, for example, smoke and develop COPD. It's creating tension and a divide in society. Your article was a breath of fresh air to read. Thank you."

# 5. Reactions from physicians

In response to the increasing social polarization surrounding the COVID-19 vaccination, numerous doctors from around the world have contacted me to share their thoughts. This chapter offers an in-depth look at the voices from medical practice and raises the question of how far society is prepared to accept different opinions.

## A physician from the USA

"Thank you for your comments in the Lancet regarding the stigmatization of Covid unvaccinated individuals. You are brave to speak out. Know that there are many of us—physicians like myself as well as laypeople—who stand with you."

## A pulmonologist from the USA

"Thank you for that terrific letter. I am glad The Lancet would print such a thing; no US journal or "respectable" newspaper in the US would."

## A pathologist from Canada

"Thank you for providing your expertise and sharing your knowledge and would like to thank you for your support. I have been stigmatized, and have been excluded from my hospital and work (as an unjabbed despite natural immunity, and being asymptomatic) and despite helping about 10,000 patients in the last two years during these difficult times. I have been forced off work and I am currently unpaid for almost two months. This is despite training for almost twenty years.

I was allowed to enter and work until unpaid to help my patients (and have been now for almost two months) however when I entered on another day with a pre-sent email notice, negative rapid test (entering again without any symptoms, confirmed on entry with security/staff) and natural immunity I was suspended. I even had submitted a documented letter and also a valid medical exemption signed by my family doctor. The hospital chief of staff escorted me out with threats of security escort, with a verbal reporting of suspension and follow-up email of suspension notice suggesting that I could cause people harm / injury: "Your failure to comply exposes or is reasonably likely to expose patients, health care providers, employees or others you come into contact with at the Hospital to harm."

This is despite the fact that I only work on glass slides on a microscope, in a private office with HEPA (high efficiency particulate air; addition by the author) filtration and can work from home. The only harm I see is the further delays to surgeries and diagnosis as no one will be able to cover my almost 5000 cases per year, and we were already at least one - two people short. The hospital has refused to accommodate me. I have never directly worked with patients for over three years, and only communicate to staff as a consultant mainly through email/zoom/telephone with no close contacts. I also videotaped my entry into the hospital to my private office showing this.

I am currently out of work for almost two months and have kids and a wife to support financially as the only bread winner. Please let me know your thoughts about this situation. I do not believe I am a risk to anyone considering the availability of the "vaccines" and first line therapies to any one in need. At my hospital we had hardly any COVID cases. In fact, all the recent six cases in that region are all in vaccinated individuals. We have had major delays to biopsies and surgeries and their diagnosis which is causing significant harms to patients and untimely deaths."

## An emergency physician from Germany (translated)

"Thank you very much for your well-written article in The Lancet. It is good to meet colleagues who are not only professional enough to deal with content objectively (as we should do in scientific discourse), but who also do not forget the human aspects."

## A physician from Germany (translated)

"Thank you for your important article in the Lancet entitled 'COVID-19: stigmatising the unvaccinated is not justified'. It really is about time someone pointed this out."

## An oncologist from Germany (translated)

"I would like to express my relief and the support I feel for your current position in the Lancet. You are certainly being inundated at the moment, but I would like to ask whether we should not sensibly endeavour to create a kind of network of all those who are critical of the current development in order to gain a clearer voice and make the counterweight visible in these dangerous times."

A physician from Germany (translated)

"Thank you very much for your clear words, which I read in The Lancet, and with which you take the side of the wrongly accused unvaccinated!"

A physician from Germany (translated)

"I would like to congratulate you on your publication in the Lancet and thank you for the clarity with which you address this highly topical issue of stigma and division in our society. I hope that your article will be heard, including by those with political responsibility. It would be great if you could be invited onto TV programmes and discuss this topic with Mr Lauterbach, Mr Söder, Mr Kretschmann, Mr Wieler and Mr Spahn, for example, as objectively and clearly as you did in your article."

A cardiologist from the USA

"Glad to see people finally speaking out again the preposterous discrimination against those who are not vaccinated. To your point, consider that one regional US health care system I know of currently requires employees or medical staff granted exemptions from vaccination to have WEEKLY Covid testing. Fully vaccinated personnel have no requirement as if they pose no risk of transmission. This weekly testing is a part of Biden's upcoming broad mandate. It makes no sense and is clearly punitive to coerce individuals to get vaccinated.

Unfortunately, for those who do not know any better, it promotes prejudice and unwarranted division. I hope Germany is not as crazy as the US!"

## A vascular surgeon from the USA

"Thank you for your Lancet correspondence on stigmatizing the unvaccinated. The pandemic should be taking a new approach of personalized risk assessment based upon breakthrough infections and transmission by vaccinated individuals. Mandates are illogical if vaccinated individuals can shed and spread the virus. Public health needs a more broad box of tools to counter the delta variant than only vaccines. Therapeutics must be included and emphasized. The epidemiology of breakthrough infections must be collected and it must be reported in a transparent way so people make informed personal decisions. And, as you said, we must stop negatively stigmatizing the unvaccinated."

## A physician from Germany (translated)

"I read your recently published Correspondence Letters in the Lancet with great pleasure and extreme interest. I would like to thank you from the bottom of my heart for your clarity and courage! Unfortunately, this courage is also necessary at the moment, as I have to realise with a somewhat tearful face. Please allow me to say that you are one of the 'mavericks' of hygiene, so to speak - I write this with admiration, as I think that courageous and clear-thinking people like you will be very important for the future of hygiene. I hope that my little

message has given you some extra energy and reassur-
ance!"

A physician from Germany (translated)

"I would like to thank you very much for your courageous and sincere letter to the editors of The Lancet.
Such a communication was long overdue. In fact, it is
almost an incitement to hatred that is being expressed
by politicians against the scientific findings that I follow."

A neurologist from Germany (translated)

"I would like to thank you for your recent article in the
Lancet. You speak from the heart. It is wrong to look for
the solution to this pandemic in vaccination alone and
the resulting stigmatisation of the unvaccinated. The
pandemic is being driven by many factors and we must
therefore take a multifactorial approach. Vaccination is
a major part of this, but it is not the only factor. In recent
months, I have been very concerned about social developments and increasing radicalisation, including
among doctors. I experienced this myself when I criticised the 2G regulation for visitors to the hospital to the
managing director. I criticised the fact that not only
could potentially infected people bring the infection into
the hospital in an uncontrolled manner, but that people
were also being denied access to their sick relatives. This
de facto safeguarding of the unvaccinated led to a veri-
table tirade of hatred from the medical profession, to
whom my letter had been forwarded in the meantime,
and my boss was urged to remove me from the hospital's

consultation service. I find such reactions extremely worrying."

## A physician from Norway

"Thank you from the bottom of my heart for you article about stigmatising the unvaccinated. I was so happy to hear a German voicing this. I was a medical student in Germany and now work as an ophthalmologist in Norway. I am so worried when I talk on the phone with some of my German friends, and they do not see the danger at all in what language they talk about the unvaccinated. They don't want to listen to me when I say that the vaccinated spread the virus too. My parents where young students in the second World War. It is not that far back. We must be aware of the danger in treating parts of the population as unclean. People in Norway of course talk like that too, it seems to be appropriate as long as our leaders and journalists support that kind of language. We must fight for the human dignity in language and behaviour."

## A physician

"I am a medical doctor (outside Germany). I have been really worried about the worldwide movement to make COVID-19 vaccination mandatory and the stigmatization of unvaccinated people, as I think basic human rights are harassed. I am also suspicious of the quality of information spread. In an effort to obtain an objective view on the topic, I searched COVID-19-related information on PubMed. Information is explicitly in favour of covid vaccination and unvaccinated people are considered the cause of COVID spread. Then, I came across your articles. I agree with you. I also agree with what you write in your last paper (which seems that has been withdrawn). I had observed that the new surge in COVID-19 cases took place after the government instructions (in many countries) that vaccinated people could go back to life as in the precovid era: vaccinated people did not wear masks and did not follow basic social distancing rules, whereas unvaccinated people were excluded for social activities, thus the latter could not be the cause of the new surge. There was a period during the summer and autumn that people did not follow any covid-related restrictions. Governments were at least irresponsible to say that vaccinated people would need no restrictions. I think that the fanaticism and "efforts" for stigmatization of anyone who has a different opinion are dangerous and have made me suspicious of what is really going on. At the early stages of the pandemic, I was in favour of COVID vaccination, now the situation sounds to me at least strange and I have become suspicious of the vaccination itself. People will lose their jobs, and in some countries, they will pay monthly penalties (>60 yo, Greece: penalty 100 euros/month when basic salary is ~500 euros) for choosing not to vaccinate. Also, people would have to be vaccinated every 3-4 months to be protected. What is going on? Is there any possibility that scientific information is biased to encourage COVID vaccination for some reason (that I cannot understand at this moment)? I face ethical issues every day and I feel really awkward with the situation. What could we do to reverse this situation? We are

moving back from individualized medicine to massive
medicine and medieval attitudes."

25

# 6. Reactions from professors

Several professors from around the world have contacted me to criticize the stigmatisation of the unvaccinated as dangerous and divisive. Their emails reflect a deep concern about societal trends and the consequences of a one-sided political agenda. This chapter summarizes their views and highlights the ethical and scientific concerns behind this discussion.

A professor from Germany (translated)

"Thank you for the thoughtful letter in the Lancet. I am completely with you. The noticeable insecurity of the population and the sometimes aggressive reaction is probably influenced to a considerable extent by this stigmatisation."

A professor from the USA

"Thank you for writing the powerful letter to The Lancet. I much appreciated your words, and welcome another voice in this madness."

A professor from France

"I just read your letter to the Lancet and want to congratulate you. I am of course pro-vaccine (and vaccinated with three doses since January) but it is good to remind everyone of the dark sides of our history (you mention US and Germany) but France also has had — and still has – its deviancies."

"Thank you for your very nice and informative article in the 'Lancet' on the subject of corona and vaccination, especially for the fact-based presentation of the high risk of disease in vaccinated people compared to unvaccinated people. I am sure you are also familiar with the statistical study from Thuringia on the correlation between vaccination incidence and disease frequency in German federal states: Saxony and Thuringia as corona 'hotspots' currently have by far the lowest vaccination rates. Unfortunately, given the attitude of our politicians with regard to vaccination protection without testing - considered sufficient during 2G to prevent the spread - it is to be feared that infection rates will continue to rise significantly in the coming weeks. A few tens of thousands of spectators in football stadiums last week, most of them probably vaccinated but not tested (2G), were apparently not a problem. However, unvaccinated people with a negative test are increasingly being declared pariahs and excluded from public life. This is possibly fuelling an already subliminal pogrom mood towards unvaccinated people among medical laypeople and driving a division in society. Unfortunately, the opinions of our specialist colleagues are just as varied as the virus mutations. And not a word has been said about the risks of vaccination. Thank you again for your article."

## A professor from Bulgaria

"I congratulate you on your dignified position as a healer and human being and I assure you that you are not alone in your understanding expressed in your publication "COVID-19: stigmatizing the unvaccinated is not justified"."

## A retired professor from the USA

"Congratulations on a magnificent article in The Lancet about the unvaccinated. This is an important addition to the global body of knowledge about this disease. Thank you for getting the data and reporting the data in this very high-profile journal. It will have a large impact. Well done."

## A professor from Germany (translated)

"Thank you for your courageous letter in LANCET regarding the stigmatisation of unvaccinated people! Your article in the Ärzteblatt about (virtually non-existent) surface transmission is also spectacular, culminating in your sentence: "However, regular surface disinfection reduces the diversity of the microbiome and increases the diversity of resistance genes." It would be good if more successful doctors shared their expertise with the public. It can't be that we are only informed by Lauterbach, Wieler and Drosten! It's good to know that there are still sensible scientists out there! I can't go too far out on a limb here, I'm the only one of 25 colleagues who is still somewhat civilised. Everyone else nods uncritically at everything that comes out of Berlin via its media. How far have we come in Germany? If nothing is questioned and (sometimes) controversially discussed, even at universities, then our society has reached a dead end that it has declared a one-way street."

# 7. Reactions from scientists

Some scientists and experts warned of the danger of fostering social division and hostility, while the focus should be on cooperation and rational solutions. Their emails shed light on the far-reaching consequences of political decisions and call for a differentiated view of the epidemiological situation.

### A university scientist from Austria (translated)

"Thank you very much for your courageous letter and your statement."

### A scientist from Germany (translated)

"I would like to thank you for having the courage to make what I believe to be a correct and necessary appeal, which is not exactly popular. I refer to your article of November 2021 'COVID-19: stigmatising the unvaccinated is not justified'. I find it extremely worrying in these difficult times to incite hatred against a section of the population, in this case the unvaccinated. Regardless of the effectiveness of the vaccine, we should all be working together to fight the virus. Division and hatred are definitely not the way forward for society."

### A scientist from Germany (translated)

"I have read your article 'COVID-19: stigmatising the unvaccinated is not justified' in The Lancet and would like to express my sincere thanks. As a (non-specialist) scientist, I sincerely hope that with this article and the letter 'The epidemiological relevance of the COVID-19-vaccinated population is increasing', also in The Lancet, you can make a contribution to a truly sensible and rational approach to Covid-19 in society and politics. Personally, I think that the way politicians are going about dealing with Covid-19, with increasing pressure on the unvaccinated and the threat of compulsory vaccination as the only way out, is very dangerous and unjustified. At the same time, I am very irritated that the increasing excess mortality in Germany and the UK is not being addressed in the media and by politicians. Do you have an explanation for this excess mortality?"

A data analyst from Ireland

"I have read your Lancet article (COVID-19: stigmatising the unvaccinated is not justified) with great interest and you couldn't be more right. The authorities are blaming the unvaccinated for the sun not rising in the morning. From publicly available data published by the Irish Health Protection Surveillance Centre, I can see that in Oct-Nov 80%+ of the cases and deaths have been in vaccinated individuals. Ireland is about 92% vaccinated at this stage. So the infestation/mortality follow the vaccination rate closely enough."

# 8. Reactions from students

Students from the UK and Germany have written to me to criticize the stigmatisation of the unvaccinated and the impact of political decisions on society. Their letters reflect not only their concerns about the current situation, but also their vision of a more rational, compassionate and enlightened future. This chapter highlights the moving and often courageous thoughts of a generation navigating between science, politics and ethics in the midst of the pandemic.

## A student from Germany (translated)

"I just wanted to say thank you for your correspondence article in the Lancet. It must have taken a lot of courage to even write this piece, which goes against the guidance of the government, and against the corporate social media, big pharma, and narrative of the public media. I sincerely hope that all your research colleagues at least support your stance! I'm a researcher at a German university myself, and I can't even say in front of my left-leaning colleagues that I believe the vaccinated should *not* be ostracised, excluded from public life, or barred from studying or working. They all think that the unvaccinated should pay their own health bills and lose their jobs if they don't comply! What happened to tolerance and compassion? It's really frightening what I am seeing, and these are people with PhDs. I'm glad to see that level-headed scientists like you are at least looking at the data and trying to unite the country again."

A student from Germany (translated)

"As a German citizen, I have asked myself many questions on this topic, especially with regard to our history, and therefore thought that your letter was right and courageous. Furthermore, I thought that your reflections, which led to the letter and its publication, were an exemplary fulfilment of your duty as a citizen and as a human being. I mean your duty to make use of your common sense and your intellect. 'Enlightenment is man's emergence from his self-imposed immaturity' wrote Kant and I had to think of this when I read your letter. P.S. You may be interested to know that I am a young and vaccinated student. I think it is a good idea (as far as science can prove today) to make use of the vaccine, but I can only wholeheartedly agree with the last two sentences of your letter, because there are far more dangerous things than a deadly virus."

A student from the UK

"I am a fourth year Pharmacy student, with a special interest in public health. Next year I am due to begin my pre-registration training as a Junior Pharmacist. I have read, among other works, your inspiring piece, "COVID-19: stigmatising the unvaccinated is not justified". The direction in which political agendas are moving are deeply worrying to me too. Mostly, I felt moved to write and say thank you personally for bringing to light an insidious stigmatisation by many governments and medias, and the fitting reminder at the end for us all "to put an extra effort into putting society together". Something that is going on in the United Kingdom is, despite huge national shortages of doctors, nurses etc., many healthcare professionals have been fired due to their vaccination 'status'. Yet, reportedly, as pressure mounts on the creaking system with more cases of Omicron, vaccinated staff who have tested positively are even being asked to come back to work without delay. I am so grateful to see awareness of this issue being raised."

## 9. Reactions from psychologists

Psychologists from two countries offer an insightful analysis of the social impact of the pandemic in their emails. They address the moral responsibility of science and the media, the psychological mechanisms behind stigmatisation and the dangers of mass influence. Their voices open up a discussion about the psychological consequences of the political and social decisions of those years and their long-term effects on the collective good.

A psychologist from the UK

"I want to thank you for having the courage to speak sense and truth at a time when scientists are being muzzled and people are being negatively influenced by - what I believe to be - mass hypnosis. Indeed, I speak from experience because I am a certified hypnotherapist with a diploma in hypnotherapy. The psychological head games that they are playing are immoral and irresponsible. This type of stigmatization did not end well in Nazi Germany."

A psychologist from Germany (translated)

"I hope that you will not suffer any personal disadvantages as a result of your correspondence in the Lancet."

## 10. Reactions from nurses

Three emails were received from nurses, expressing grat-
itude for the content of my letter. Below I share thoughts
of one nurse anonymously.

### A nurse from Canada

"Thanks for the article and the call for reason. Very
much appreciated your words. Don't stop."

# 11. Other reactions

In this chapter, various experts have their say, critically examining the political and social developments of the pandemic in their emails. Whether lawyers, politicians or health professionals - they all emphasize the need for a rational and fair debate. Their concerns about the marginalization of the unvaccinated and the creation of a social climate of division raise important questions that should not go unanswered in a democratic society.

### A lawyer from Germany (translated)

"Thank you for your article. I am also trying to make sure that reason and humanity prevail and that an open scientific discussion takes place again. We are currently causing a fundamental damage to all our foundations. The system is attacking itself in a quasi-autoimmune way at the level of law and ethics. Values and foundations are being reduced to absurdity."

### A pharmacist from Canada

"Thank you very much for your article. Working in a hospital gave me this chance to observe the consequences of this stigma. Even from the beginning, all published information were inconclusive regarding the risk unvaccinated people would cause in comparison with an asymptomatic vaccinated carrier of the virus. Since in our facilities, due to the shortage of health care workers and the cost of the frequent testing, massive testing has never been an option, the real infection rate in healthcare workers is unknown. False negative tests are an additional problem. Stigmatizing the unvaccinated is not only not appropriate but also scientifically wrong. Our policies are preventing an individual with symptoms to attend work or any other public place. But an vaccinated asymptomatic who carries the same load of virus (as we already know), can expose more risk by attending work....., since that individual is unaware of his infection. Thank you again for voicing your concerns."

## A senator from Italy

"We were very impressed with your article published in The Lancet about the "pandemic of the unvaccinated". This is an issue that is very close to our hearts and we are also dealing with at the political level in recent weeks."

## A human rights campaigner from Germany (translated)

"Thank you very much for your article in the Lancet, it is so depressing to see how the tone of the media and politics is bringing out the lowest instincts in the population. I am very worried, not for myself, but for my grandchildren who will have to bear the brunt of all the bad decisions being made at the moment. It makes me sick that I can't protect them from it."

## An osteopath from Germany (translated)

"I would like to thank you very much for your voice in these times. Your recent Lancet articles should get your place in the media headlines. A few weeks ago, I had a conversation with a professor about the consequences of excluding the unvaccinated. His research findings on mass psychological phenomena do not bode well if this trend is consolidated in the media and politics. Thank you very much for your overview and consistency at this time."

## 12. The reaction from my university

As an external scientist, I have been an associate professor of hygiene and environmental medicine at the University of Greifswald since 2009. But at the end of 2021, there were apparently self-imposed taboos in the thinking in parts of the scientific community. On 14 December 2021, I received an official email with the following content, which I quote here in part:

> *"In order to avoid future damage to our image, I must ask you to submit articles with the affiliation ... to me for approval in any case, in order to prevent scientifically untenable statements such as the last two letters from you in the Lancet with the Greifswald affiliation from appearing. As we cannot allow the statements you have made to stand, because they could lead to unacceptable uncertainty, we will write a reply."*

An article that has to be approved by a university representative before submission? This can be seen as attempted preventive censorship. I had always thought that the freedom of science was secure in Germany. Preventive censorship could only exist in countries like North Korea, but not in Germany! Obviously, I was wrong.

And it was apparently not even considered necessary to explain to me exactly which specific publications were involved and which of the statements were considered "scientifically untenable". If they were the "last two letters in The Lancet", it would have been the one on the unjustified stigmatisation of the unvaccinated and an article of 4 February 2021, in which Martin Kulldorff and I called for a careful evaluation of the benefits and risks of the COVID-19 measures [6].

But perhaps all the Lancet journals were meant? In this case, it would have been the letter on the unjustified stigmatisation of the unvaccinated and a letter in The Lancet Regional Health – Europe on the partly incorrect argumentation of the Leopoldina to justify another lockdown [7], a letter that was retracted on 12 January 2022 because of the publication of a previous version of this paper by the publisher [8]. Whatever the university representative meant, I was not told which two of the published papers caused so much concern, nor was I told what exactly was considered to be "scientifically untenable statements" leading to "image damage" and "unacceptable uncertainty".

I sought advice from trusted colleagues at other universities and was able to present my concerns to a constitutional lawyer. He helped me to assess whether, as an external person with the title of associate professor at the university, I was covered by the academic freedom protected by the German constitution. This is the statement:

*"The first question that arises under the constitution is whether you are the holder of academic freedom (Article 5 (3) sentence 1, Grundgesetz). There can be no serious doubt about this, since you have habilitated and have the status of an adjunct professor at the University of Greifswald, which means that you have been entrusted with the independent representation of an academic subject (cf. BVerfGE 35, p. 79 [112]; p. 95, 193 [209]).*

*The second question concerns the specific protection they enjoy. The following applies here: According to case-law, the scientific aspect of research (Article 5.3 sentence 1 of the Grundgesetz) protects in particular the free, i.e. independent and self-determined choice of questions and methods, the entire practical implementation of a research project as well as the evaluation and dissemination of the research results (BVerfGE 35, 79 [113]). No state authority, not even the university and its self-governing bodies, may interfere with the scientist's freedom to take his or her own scientific initiative and to choose and carry out his or her research project (BVerfGE 57, 70 [95]). This also includes the fact that departments may not make official statements on the quality of the scientific activity of an individual university lecturer (BVerwGE 102, 304 [312]).*

*Applying these rules to your case, it must be concluded that a publication in the medical journal Lancet is a scientific publication in the required sense. The department may therefore not prevent you from publishing on your own initiative and in a self-determined manner, stating your academic institution ("affiliation"). In particular, they may not order a prior 'submission for approval' (i.e. censorship). Finally, he or she may not officially comment on your publications by writing a 'reply' and thus discredit them.*

*Of course, this does not preclude a professional rebuttal by colleagues in a publication equivalent to yours, for example in the Lancet or another scientific journal. This would be the proper way of scientific debate on technical issues and - if I may say so - the only proper way of avoiding 'intolerable uncertainty' among the public about current events in the field of science."*

On 27 December 2021, I replied to the email of the university representative and wrote the following text:

*"I consider a request of this kind to be unusual, as normally the editors of scientific journals evaluate a scientific paper, including letters to the editor, on the basis of expert opinions and then make a decision regarding publication. After an initial assessment, I consider myself to be a holder of academic freedom according to the constitution, as I hold the status of an associate professor at the University of Greifswald ..., which means that I have been assigned the independent representation of an academic field. Consequently, I consider the free, i.e. independent and self-determined choice of questions and topics for publication to be protected. As far as I am aware, the university may not interfere with the freedom of academic initiative guaranteed to the academic. For me, the request is therefore in contradiction to the academic freedom enshrined in the constitution; I see it as preventive or pre-censorship. From now on, I am happy to add a disclaimer to manuscripts that makes it clear that it is personal point of view: "The views expressed here are those of the author and do not necessarily reflect those of his university." This leaves the possibility that the university may represent a different point of view to the outside world."*

A day later I got the answer:

*"Whether a footnote "The views expressed here are those of the author and do not necessarily reflect those*

*of his university" is sufficient if a political view, which is also backed up with scientifically incorrect statements, that contradicts the view of the ..., I cannot judge from a legal perspective. I am therefore forwarding the correspondence to our legal department with a request for clarification."*

I was promised that I would be contacted after the legal clarification, but I have not received a reply for almost three years. Presumably, the legal department did not see a clear case to support the university representative's attempted preventive censorship.

On 5 January 2022 I received a message from the editor of The Lancet Regional Health – Europe. I was told that the office had received a correspondence in response to my previous letters. This was the first time that I had been told which of my letters was the cause of concern. It was the letter about the inappropriate stigmatisation of the unvaccinated in The Lancet, and another piece based on official data from the Robert Koch Institute to show that the epidemiological relevance of the COVID-19 vaccinated was increasing, published in The Lancet Regional Health - Europe [9]. My colleague's submission was rejected at this stage, the editors felt that their piece was a gross misinterpretation to counter my letter. The editor wrote:

*"The bottom-line message of both the published Letters from Dr. Kampf is that we should take into account vaccinated people as the source of infection—which is that fact, as we know that vaccinated people can still transmit the virus, and be infected.".*

This is exactly what I tried to describe in both letters, not only the unvaccinated are possible sources of transmission, but some of my colleagues read it in a completely different way.

Even if it had "only" been the expression of an opinion in a scientific journal that is quite obviously factually incorrect, it would still fall under freedom of opinion. Article 5 paragraph 1 sentence 1 of the German Constitution states: "Everyone has the right to freely express and disseminate his opinions in speech, writing and pictures and to inform himself without hindrance from generally accessible sources."

On November 28, 2011, the Federal Constitutional Court handed down a landmark ruling on freedom of opinion in accordance with Article 5, Paragraph 1, Sentence 1 of the German constitution [10]. It states:

*"The scope of protection of freedom of opinion includes, on the one hand, opinions, i.e. statements characterized by the element of comment and opinion. They always fall within the scope of protection of Article 5 (1) sentence 1 of the Constitution, regardless of whether they prove to be true or untrue, whether they are justified or unfounded, emotional or rational, or whether they are considered valuable or worthless, dangerous or harmless. They do not lose this protection even if they are expressed sharply and exaggeratedly."*

This experience had a lasting effect on my view of academic freedom at universities. There were university academics who wanted to check and ultimately decide whether my manuscripts for scientific journals were acceptable to their personal standards. I had previously trusted in controversy and debate among colleagues and saw the university as the last great bastion in defence of academic freedom. I now experienced an attempt to stifle controversy and debate and, ultimately, academic freedom.

## 13. Two reactions published in the Lancet

In response to my Lancet correspondence, two letters to the editor were published in the Lancet.

A university ethicist from the USA

A response to my letter was written by Arthur Caplan, who was affiliated with the Division of Medical Ethics, New York University, USA. He saw the unvaccinated as morally accountable and responsible for behaviour that leads to or causes preventable harm. He wrote [11]:

*"Criticising those who, through their non-vaccination, wind up in hospitals and morgues in huge numbers, put stress on finite resources, and prolong the pandemic by permitting higher rates of viral transmission, is not stigmatising, it is deserved moral condemnation. Those who do not get vaccinated harm not only themselves but also their communities. That is inappropriate, selfish behaviour."*

In his view, the unvaccinated would be more likely to be hospitalized or die, while the vaccinated would be less likely to be hospitalized or die. However, this view ignores the fact that it is not the entire population that will benefit from a COVID-19 vaccination, but mostly some groups at increased risk. It also ignores the harm that can be caused by COVID-19 vaccines, including severe auto-immune disease and death. And it ignores the natural immunity that provides better protection against a SARS-CoV-2 infection.

Another view is that the unvaccinated will prolong the pandemic by allowing higher rates of viral transmission, although Caplan did not even provide a reference to support his claim. This view was very popular in 2021 and was repeated many times by some politicians and scientists, but it did not turn out to be correct. Neither the viral load, nor the duration of viral shedding, nor the secondary transmission rates provided consistent and convincing evidence that the risk of transmission to contact persons was higher among the unvaccinated. Therefore, this statement by Caplan could be considered questionable in 2021 and can be considered incorrect today [12].

If a citizen considers his risk of severe or critical COVID-19 to be low, and if the same person considers himself to be at risk of a severe adverse event following vaccination, it is neither inappropriate nor selfish not to be vaccinated. The World Medical Association writes in the Medical Ethics Manual in 2015:

*"The patient has the right to self-determination, to make free decisions regarding himself/herself. The physician will inform the patient of the consequences of his/her decisions."*

Caplan apparently saw the ethical principle of self-determination as a morally condemnable, inappropriate and selfish behaviour. A view I cannot share.


## Two university scientists from Australia

A further response came from Sam Egger and Garry Egger who questioned the presentation of the numbers. They argued that in the context of COVID-19 vaccines, the base-rate fallacy is often described as the illusion that vaccines are ineffective because, in highly vaccinated populations, the majority of COVID-19 cases occur among vaccinated people [13].

This is certainly true, but it does not change the fact that a significant number of new COVID-19 cases also occurred among the fully vaccinated. And the officially published case numbers alone do not distinguish between asymptomatic, mild, moderate, severe, critical and fatal cases, a distinction that is essential for assessing medically relevant risks [14].

# 14. Tolerance

Tolerance is a fundamental element for harmonious and respectful coexistence in a society. It enables people to accept and respect different opinions, lifestyles and cultural backgrounds. Tolerance promotes dialogue and understanding between individuals, which contributes to peaceful coexistence. Without tolerance, on the other hand, a society can quickly slide into conflict and division. When intolerance towards certain groups or individuals prevails, tensions often lead to discrimination, marginalisation and even violence. Historically, such societal fractures have had serious consequences for social stability and the well-being of all citizens. Therefore, the commitment to tolerance should not only be an obligation, but also a necessity in order to maintain social peace in society.

## 14.1. Tolerance in science

Let's first look at the reactions to my Lancet letter. What was surprising about the large number of responses was that some people felt it was brave to write a letter with this content. One reader even expressed the hope that this letter would not cause me any disadvantages. Yes, at a time when the vast majority of the media and many scientists saw the unvaccinated as the greatest threat to public health, anyone who questioned this thesis was swimming against the tide.

Many doctors, scientists and university lecturers have thanked me for this short article. It did me good and was completely unexpected. Equally unexpected was the reaction of a representative of the University of Greifswald, who attempted preventive censorship. The constitution protects the freedom of science. As a bearer of this freedom in my function as an associate professor, I am free to choose and publish topics and texts, as long as the editors of the journals accept the texts for publication. The university has no right to interfere or censor. And yet they have tried. It is frightening!

If the person who asked me to ask for permission prior to submitting my manuscripts had embraced the spirit of academic freedom, he would never have made this attempt, but would have communicated to the outside world with deep conviction that he himself, out of professional conviction, held a different point of view and would introduce it into the discussion, but that he was standing protectively in front of me because, after all, controversy is part of science, and so is the publication of different points of view in the journals. But these colleagues were very far from this sovereign position in the spirit of scientific freedom. There was an authoritarian, almost totalitarian spirit in this attempt.

And the academic freedom is still in danger. Here is an example from 2024: A Dutch working group describes excess mortality in 47 countries between 2020 and 2022 in the journal BMJ Public Health. Only in the discussion of the study is it vaguely suggested that the COVID-19 vaccination may have contributed to this. The paper was published on 3 June 2024 [15]. As early as 11 June 2024, the Princess Máxima Center, where the first author works, distanced itself from this publication and expressed its deep regret that this publication could give the impression that the importance of COVID-19 vaccination could be called into question [16].

And why does an employer, for whom the freedom of science should apply, distance itself from the content of a publication by its own employees? The appropriate way would have been to write and submit a letter to the editor explaining, on the basis of comprehensible reasons, why other scientists have a different point of view.

Academic freedom in the European Union was last assessed in 2023. Eight out of nine countries with below-average levels of academic freedom have experienced a statistically significant decline in academic freedom over the past decade, indicating an erosion of this important fundamental academic value [17]. This finding is consistent with my personal experience.

Walter Hirsch wrote in 1961 [18]:

*"Totalitarian societies seek to implement their goals by maximum politization of life, e.g. by stressing the relevance of ALL behaviour for the social goals, which have been largely determined by political authority, and be severely restricting individual choices considered antagonistic or irrelevant to these goals. The means for this include ideological indoctrination, centralized planning, the leadership principle, and the breaking up of "private" groups and institutions considered socially harmful."*

In 2021, the majority of scientists, politicians and media supported the goal of achieving the highest possible COVID-19 vaccination rate. This goal was largely determined by political authority and was supported in parallel by severely restricting individual choices (such as widespread restrictions of public life opportunities in Germany for the unvaccinated; "2G").

The public and repeated stigmatisation of the unvaccinated can be seen as ideological indoctrination, the leadership principle can be found in the attempted preventive censorship in science. My words in the Lancet letter were described in one email as potentially leading to "unacceptable uncertainty", Hirsch used the phrase "socially harmful".

There are indeed some parallels between the characteristics of totalitarian systems described by Hirsch and the treatment of the unvaccinated and the dealing with dissenters during the pandemic in 2021.

---

**Issac Asimov (1988)**
"The saddest aspect of life right now is that science gathers knowledge faster than society gathers wisdom."

---

*14.2. Tolerance in the society*

Tolerance towards those who think differently is becoming increasingly rare. This was very evident during the intense phase of the pandemic. But how did this happen?

People often respond to threats with generalisations caused by a misjudgement of risk, a selective choice of their information or an unwillingness to update their own beliefs based on new information. We now know that these processes have led some people to use a single piece of information - COVID-19 vaccination status - as a heuristic to make judgements about the culpability of individuals. It did not matter whether they were statistically more likely to need medical care, posed a serious threat to the health of others, had already recovered from the infection, or how long it had been since their last booster vaccination.

These exaggerated generalisations and the resulting scapegoating have not been without consequences. One social consequence of this is that these 'scapegoats' can be ostracised, discriminated against and, in extreme cases, even confronted with violence and persecution [19]. Why did so many people put up with this?

A Danish team studied the discriminatory attitudes of vaccinated and unvaccinated people in the USA during the pandemic [20]. In addition to feelings of antipathy, several fundamental freedoms were assessed. Vaccinated people showed a significantly stronger discriminatory attitudes towards unvaccinated people (+7% to +28%) on all questions about fundamental rights and freedoms. Unvaccinated people, on the other hand, only felt significantly more antipathy towards vaccinated people (+4%), but this was low compared to vaccinated people (+16%). For all questions on fundamental rights and freedoms, the unvaccinated showed no discriminatory attitudes towards the vaccinated. At these rates, the negative attitudes of the vaccinated towards the unvaccinated were even stronger than their negative attitudes towards atheists and former prisoners or drug addicts.

Parents who chose not to vaccinate their children against COVID-19 were also stigmatised. In Australia, for example, 21 parents from regional and urban areas in five states were interviewed. Their experiences point to systematic stigma. Parents experienced labelling. They also experienced stereotyping, with many not identifying with the 'anti-vaxxers' portrayed in the media and describing frustration at being labelled as such, believing they were protecting their child from harm. Participants described social 'othering' leading to loss of relationships and social isolation. They described status loss and discrimination, feeling 'dismissed' as incompetent parents and discriminated against by medical professionals and other parents. Finally, changes in legislation exerted power over their circumstances, making it impossible for them to provide their children with the same financial and educational opportunities as vaccinated children, often increasing their steadfastness in refusing vaccination [21].

Similar results would probably have been achieved in Germany. Repeated negative remarks about the unvaccinated, such as 'crazy people' (Joachim Gauck, former German President), 'dangerous social pests' (Rainer Stinner, FDP politician) or 'antisocial idiots' (Christoph Waltz, actor and two-time Oscar winner), may have contributed to this discriminatory attitude of the vaccinated towards the unvaccinated. Is this really how we want to think about each other and subsequently talk in public? Language has power, and no-one should underestimate this when denigrating their counterparts.

Unvaccinated people have been widely blamed for prolonging the pandemic. The first notion does not hold up when examined in light of the data until 2022, which finds no correlation between percentage of the population vaccinated and Covid infections [22]. We have at least a *prima facie* reason not to assume that, if only more people (i.e., a greater percentage of populations) were to get vaccinated, then the pandemic would be over.

The end of a pandemic was, in any case, a political decision, without a clear-cut or universal definition. It depends on many factors, not all epidemiological [23]. Blaming unvaccinated individuals and condemning them for prolonging a pandemic whose end is not clearly defined is misguided [1].

The controversial topics have not disappeared. Let's take the example of the war between Russia and Ukraine. Anyone who publicly speaks out in favour of a negotiated solution and rejects further deliveries of weapons to Ukraine (as these have so far only prolonged the war, increased the number of dead and injured and increased the extent of the destruction) can quickly be publicly vilified. Chancellor Olaf Scholz, for example, spoke of 'fallen angels from hell', Clemens Wergin, chief foreign affairs correspondent for the daily newspaper Welt, spoke of 'armchair pacifists' ("Lumpenpazifist"). And once again people with a different point of view are being insulted, once again society is being divided even further.

I find it particularly frightening that the negative rhetoric towards parts of the population has historical precedents. At the end of the Weimar Republic, the unemployed, disabled and chronically ill were labelled as 'ballast existences', 'parasites', 'asocials' or 'incapable of community life' [13]. Has nothing been learnt from history in this country? Is it so difficult for the protagonists of public life to be a role model in a positive sense, including in their choice of words towards those who think differently?

As for the recruitment of negative emotions and stigmatisation, consider the following two prominent examples.

The French President Emmanuel Macron declared that the nearly five million unvaccinated people in his country were "non-citizens", claiming that he wanted to offend the unvaccinated by pushing them out of public spaces [24]. This open and targeted discrimination against a large group of citizens by an elected leader is truly unprecedented and was described as morally reprehensible [1].

Canadian Prime Minister Justin Trudeau questioned whether the rest of Canada should 'tolerate' the unvaccinated, suggesting on television that people who refuse to be vaccinated are often racist and misogynist extremists [25]. While Trudeau may not have meant to imply that all unvaccinated people are racist and misogynistic, publicly associating a heterogeneous group of unvaccinated people with some of society's most undesirable beliefs and behaviours is morally problematic.

It directs people's widespread hatred and disgust for racism and misogyny - and for those guilty of them - at unvaccinated people. Even if it is true that some unvaccinated people are also racist and misogynistic, it is clearly unjustified to extend these pejorative terms to the whole group. Some vaccinated people are certainly racist and misogynistic - especially when most adults in Western societies are now fully vaccinated [1].

In 2023, the Federal Ministry of Justice quoted the following statement:

*"The Federal Government promotes a diverse, tolerant and democratic civil society. Every person has the same rights, should have the same opportunities and should be protected from discrimination."*

A first step in this direction would be for the government and its members to set a visible example, not only in terms of sexual and gender diversity, but more importantly in terms of other societal issues such as health status, scientific views and political attitudes. These issues affect far more people and therefore have much greater significance for coexistence in society.

Especially during a pandemic, when social cohesion is a crucial societal good and when well-being during and after the pandemic depends on the goodwill of many individuals, it is important for public health policy not to moralise - and to demoralise whenever and wherever necessary. Ideally, forces from the top (e.g. at the level of governments and public health institutions) can help to ensure that inappropriate moralisation of public health does not flare up at the level of the individual [1]. This would be an enormously important step in the future.

> **Karl Raimund Popper (1949)**
> "We should therefore claim, in the name of tolerance, the right not to tolerate the intolerant."

# References


1. Kraaijeveld SR, Jamrozik E. Moralization and Mismoralization in Public Health. Med Heal Care Philos 2022; 25: 655–69.

2. Kampf G. Pandemiemanagement auf dem Prüfstand - 2G. 1st ed. Norderstedt: BoD; 2023.

3. Jonas Aston. Verabredung zur Lüge. Apollo News. 2024 [cited 2024 Oct 22]. Available from: https://apollo-news.net/rki-leaks-verabredung-zur-luege/

4. Kampf G. COVID-19: stigmatising the unvaccinated is not justified. Lancet 2021; 398: 1871.

5. Altmetric. COVID-19: stigmatising the unvaccinated is not justified - overview of attention for article published in The Lancet, November 2021. 2024 [cited 2024 Oct 2]. Available from: https://www.altmetric.com/details/117182955#score

6. Kampf G, Kulldorff M. Calling for benefit-risk evaluations of COVID-19 control measures. Lancet 2021; 397: 576–7.

7. Kampf G. Analyzing pre-pandemic patterns of contacts is partly inappropriate to explain the current COVID-19 situation in Germany. Lancet Reg Heal Eur 2022; 12: 100290.

8. The editor and publisher. Withdrawal notice to: <Describing the unvaccinated as the main driver of the current COVID-19 situation in Germany should not be based on analyzing pre-pandemic patterns of contacts> <[The Lancet Regional Health Europe 12 (2022) 100290]>. Lancet Reg Heal Eur 2022; 12: 100298.

9. Kampf G. The epidemiological relevance of the COVID-19-vaccinated population is increasing. Lancet Reg Heal Eur 2021; 11: 100272.

10. Bundesverfassungsgericht. Beschluss der 1. Kammer des Ersten Senats vom 28. November 2011 - 1 BvR 917/09 - Rn. (1

- 28). Available from:
http://www.bverfg.de/e/rk20111128_1bvr091709.html

11. Caplan AL. Stigma, vaccination, and moral accountability. Lancet 2022; 399: 626–7.

12. Kampf G. Does COVID-19 Vaccination Protect Contact Persons? A Systematic Review. Hygiene 2024; 4: 23–48.

13. Egger S, Egger G. The vaccinated proportion of people with COVID-19 needs context. Lancet 2022; 399: 627.

14. Kampf G. Evidence-based pandemic management assessment - Focus: Germany. 1st ed. Ahrensburg: tredition; 2024.

15. Mostert S, Hoogland M, Huibers M, Kaspers G. Excess mortality across countries in the Western World since the COVID-19 pandemic: 'Our World in Data' estimates of January 2020 to December 2022. BMJ Public Heal 2024; 2: e000282.

16. Prinses Máxima Centrum. The Princess Máxima Center distances itself from publication Excess mortality during COVID-19 pandemic - Prinses Máxima Centrum. 2024 [cited 2024 Oct 21]. Available from:
https://www.prinsesmaximacentrum.nl/en/news-events/news/the-princess-maxima-center-distances-itself-from-publication-excess-mortality-during-covid-19-pandemic

17. European Parliamentary Research Service. EP Academic Freedom Monitor 2023. 2024 [cited 2024 Oct 7]. Available from:
https://www.europarl.europa.eu/RegData/etudes/STUD/2024/757798/EPRS_STU(2024)757798_EN.pdf

18. Hirsch W. The Autonomy of Science in Totalitarian Societies. Soc Forces 1961; 40: 15–22.

19. Graso M, Aquino K, Chen FX, Bardosh K. Blaming the unvaccinated during the COVID-19 pandemic: the roles of political ideology and risk perceptions in the USA. J Med Ethics 2024; 50: 246-252.

20. Bor A, Jørgensen F, Petersen MB. Discriminatory Attitudes Against the Unvaccinated During a Global Pandemic. Nature 2023; 613: 704–11.

21. Wiley KE, Leask J, Attwell K, Helps C, Barclay L, Ward PR, et al. Stigmatized for standing up for my child: A qualitative study of non-vaccinating parents in Australia. SSM - Popul Heal 2021; 16: 100926.

22. Subramanian S V, Kumar A. Increases in COVID-19 are unrelated to levels of vaccination across 68 countries and 2947 counties in the United States. Eur J Epidemiol 2021; 36: 1237–40.

23. Robertson D, Doshi P. The end of the pandemic will not be televised. BMJ 2021; 375: e068094.

24. Onishi N. Using Harsh Language, Macron Issues a Challenge to the Unvaccinated. New York Times 2022 [cited 2024 Oct 7]. Available from: https://www.nytimes.com/2022/01/05/world/europe/macron-france-unvaccinated.html?smtyp=cur&smid=tw-nytimes

25. Dave Naylor. Trudeau calls the unvaccinated racist and misogynistic extremists. West. Stand 2021 [cited 2024 Oct 7]. Available from: https://www.westernstandard.news/news/trudeau-calls-the-unvaccinated-racist-and-misogynistic-extremists/article_a3bacece-2e14-5b8c-bf37-eddd672205f3.html

# About the author

Günter Kampf is a textbook author, an independent specialist in hygiene and environmental medicine in Hamburg, Germany, and an adjunct professor of hygiene and environmental medicine at the University of Greifswald, Germany. He has published more than 250 scientific papers in mostly international journals, 44 book chapters and fifteen textbooks. The main scientific topics are the various aspects of hand hygiene, surface disinfection, the development of resistance to biocidal active substances in disinfectants and preventive measures in the context of the COVID-19 pandemic.

# Recommended reading

Were some public health measures such as the mask mandate, the social exclusion of the unvaccinated ("2G") and the vaccination mandate for parts of the population suitable and necessary to control the spread of SARS-CoV-2 so that the temporary restrictions of some fundamental human rights were justified? Was COVID-19 much more dangerous compared to other coronavirus or influenza virus infections? This book may be a unique opportunity to look at the evidence as complete as possible which will allow to find out if the measures were suitable and necessary to control the spread of SARS-CoV-2 and if COVID-19 was indeed as dangerous as often described.

2024, 616 pages, www.tredition.com